THE CODE.

THE EVALUATION.

THE PROTOCOLS.

STRIVING TO BECOME AN
EMINENTLY QUALIFIED HUMAN

BY JOCKO WILLINK

WITH DAVE BERKE AND SARAH ARMSTRONG

JOCKO
PUBLISHING

The Code. The Evaluation. The Protocols.
Striving to Become an Eminently Qualified Human
Published by Jocko Publishing

Jocko Willink
The Code. The Evaluation. The Protocols.
Striving to Become an Eminently Qualified Human
Downloadable via Kindle

LCCN: 2020900497
1. Mind and Body
2. Self Help

First Edish
ISBN 13: 978-0-9816188-2-1

Jockopublishing.com
Jockopodcast.com

CONTENTS

Unmitigated Daily

Discipline

in all things.

It is the only Way.

SECTION 1

THE CODE.

THE CODE.

Without an objective,
the objective will not be reached.

Without a goal,
the goal will not be achieved.

Without a standard,
the standard will not be met.

Without a mission,
the mission cannot be accomplished.

Without an ideal,
the ideal will never be realized.

Without a clear path,
The Path cannot be followed.

Yet, we, as human beings, often go through
life without any of these.

And so, we wander.

We wander aimlessly,
          moving without making progress.

Days, months, and years pass us by.

Time is wasted, which means life is wasted.

And potential is wasted.
               Our own potential, squandered.

Meandering through life, instead of becoming
who we could be — instead of attaining our
highest possible manifestation of being, we
simply become... whatever we become.

We fall short.

In so many ways, we fall short.

But this need not be our fate.
We can prevail over mediocracy.

We do that by chasing the ideal —
our ideal.

An ideal that we must define.
An ideal that we must codify in no uncertain
terms so we know what we are striving for.
We must have a code to follow.

3

THE CODE.

1. I will take care of my physical health by exercising, eating properly, and getting the rest I need to recover and rebuild. I will take care of my physical surroundings, keeping them in order.

2. I will develop myself mentally by reading, writing, drawing, building, creating, and engaging in other activities that sharpen and expand my mind.

3. I will not waste time. Time is precious.

4. I will not waste money and I will make prudent financial decisions. Money is hard to earn.

5. I will set goals that I will strive toward.

6. I will excel in my job because work is integral to life.

7. I will be humble and not allow my ego to negatively impact my decisions.

8. I will control my emotions and not allow my emotions to negatively impact my decisions.

9. I will put others before myself. I will help other people and protect those that cannot protect themselves. I will take care of my friends and family and treat other people with respect.

10. I will be ready to protect my friends and family. My gear will be ready. I will train and prepare to defend myself and others.

This Code is not perfectly suited to
everyone. But it is not unalterable.
You can modify it if needed. Customize it for
you and your life. While it isn't perfect, it
is a good place to start.

And while we may never be able to live up to
this code, we will be better for
having tried.

We will get stronger, smarter, faster.
We will build a better career.
We will be better mothers, fathers, husbands,
wives, daughters, and sons.

We will be healthier.
Our lives will be better.
And we will make the lives of those around us
better.

And to do that, we must strive.

We must strive to be better in the things
                         that matter.

The Code sets a standard,
                the highest possible standard.

The highest possible standard
                reveals and delineates
                   The Path we must follow.

WHAT IS

The Path is how you become what you want to be, who you want to be, and what the world **needs you to be.**

It is how you reach your potential.

It is The Path of Discipline that leads to Freedom.

THE PATH?

The Path is:

A war against weakness, so it leads to
                              strength.

A war against ignorance, so it leads to
                              knowledge.

A war against confusion, so it leads to
                              understanding.

The Path is your LIFE.

And so, The Path is different for everyone. It
is your goals, your dreams, what you want to
become.

The Path is YOURS.

But at the same time, much of The Path is the
same for everyone.

The Path is how you strive to become an
                    Eminently Qualified Human.

HOW DO I

Finding The Path isn't as hard as you think.
Some of it is clearly defined in The Code.
The rest of The Path comes from simple
questions you can ask yourself:

What do you care about?
Who do you want to be?
What matters most to you?
What are the most important things in your
life?

Who are the most important people in your
life and what do they need from you?

Answer those questions, then write down what
you need to do to achieve them.

Those things that you need to do, that you
are supposed to do, that you know you must
do.

FIND THE PATH?

Those things are The Path.

The Path is in your head waiting for you to
follow it.

HOW DO I STAY

Once you see The Path, you must begin to walk down it.

This can be the most difficult part of the journey — to break free from the gravitational pull of weakness, habit, and fear.

The best way to start, is to start. Don't hesitate. Don't wait. Don't analyze or plan or research.

Just start. Now.

Once you begin down The Path, you will soon realize, it is not an easy path.
The Path is fraught with obstacles and distractions.

Laziness, ego, weakness, and immediate gratification will all try to pull you off The Path every day.

You must fight them. You will even have to fight people who don't want you on The Path.

ON THE PATH?

But you can fight.
And you can win.

Every moment you are alive is made of
choices you get to make.

Little, tiny choices that alone mean
nothing, but when combined together, mean
everything.

You have to make the right choices. The
hard choices.

You have to deny immediate gratification
and pushback against weakness.

You must impose
Unmitigated Daily Discipline
in all things.

That is how you stay on The Path.
We must stay on The Path if we are to
become an Eminently Qualified Human.

But what does this Eminently Qualified Human
look like?

What are the attributes of this person?

An Eminently Qualified Human is a
person who has achieved mastery in every facet
of life.

This person has reached their full potential in
every measurable way.

This person lives The Code.

But in order for us to live The Code,
we need to clearly define its parts so that we
can evaluate our progress every day.

We need an evaluation system to grade ourselves
as we attempt to follow The Code.

And it should be hard.
The bar must be set high.
It should be near impossible.

But just in striving, we will become better.

And, we must implement discipline.

We must aim to implement
UNMITIGATED DAILY DISCIPLINE IN ALL THINGS.

IT IS THE ONLY WAY.

There are countless aspects of life, each with a varying level of importance.
But what are the most important?
What aspects of life should be focused on?
Where should the pursuit of excellence be concentrated?

It's easy to say that everyone's life is different and that it is impossible to quantify categories that are the most important.
But that isn't true.
There are some things in life which should be universally placed in the forefront of our efforts as human beings.

To that end, here are the most critical parts of being an Eminently Qualified Human, and how they should be measured. This is how we set a standard.

This is The Code Evaluation:

SECTION 2

THE EVALUATION.

1.0 HEALTH

Since our physical bodies are the support mechanism for our brains, physical fitness and health are paramount to our existence. To be able to engage in the critical aspects of life, our bodies need to be able to endure the demands we place on them. We need to exercise, be well rested, and well-nourished to reach optimal health. On top of cardiovascular health, a person must be strong, fast, agile, flexible, and mobile. To be each of those things, you have to engage in activities that positively impact all of them. What we put into our bodies and how effectively we rest our bodies play an equally important role in ensuring we can perform at the highest level. You can't reach your potential if you aren't healthy.

1.1 PHYSICAL FITNESS

Being physically fit allows you to perform daily functions, from working, to playing with your kids, to moving things around the house — all while avoiding injury. Having an effective fitness routine when you're young sets the foundation for being fit later in life. Maintaining your physical fitness becomes more critical as you get older. This is a basic daily necessity.

1.2 SLEEP/REST

Brain and body recovery is rooted in sleep. As scientific studies on the effects of sleep continue to mount, it's becoming more and more evident that you must consistently get your required amount of sleep in order to cognitively perform on the highest levels. Sleeping too little, or too much, have dramatically negative effects on your body and ability to perform. Establish the amount of sleep you need and prioritize accordingly.

1.3 DIET/NUTRITION

There is no part of you that your diet does not affect. The fuel for your body determines how it looks, feels, and functions. Knowledge and implementation of what constitutes a healthy diet is imperative and will make the difference between maximal performance and substandard performance.

2.0 PERSONAL DEVELOPMENT

Much like our need to nourish and grow our bodies, our brains and personal behaviors need the same attention. Our brains need activities like reading, writing, building, creative pursuits, and other actions that promote intellectual health. We also need to train ourselves to improve how we deal with the challenges in our personal world. Making the best use of our limited time and money and setting goals all contribute to personal development.

2.1 INTELLECTUAL FITNESS

While carried in the chassis of the body, the mind is supreme. It is us. It needs to be protected, nourished, and trained. You exercise the brain and make it more capable by reading, writing, studying, and learning new things. You need to develop in areas that don't always fit into normal routine. Even if your job or responsibilities don't demand it, cultivate something artistic like music, writing, or singing. Do things you're not good at and try activities that make you uncomfortable. They promote creativity and intellectual growth.

2.2 TIME MANAGEMENT

There is no more valuable resource in life than time and it is limited in quantity. No one knows how much time they have, so you have to maximize all of it. ALL OF IT. And yet people waste their most precious resource every day. How well you manage your time determines how productive you are.

2.3 FINANCIAL MANAGEMENT

Like time, money is a precious resource. So avoid wasting money on anything that isn't productive. Track what you spent money on, what you saved, and what you invested. If you are disciplined with your money, you will have more of it to spend on the things you want, when you need them.

2.4 PERSONAL GOALS

You have to know what your objectives are to put meaning around the things you are doing. Set physical goals like running a 5K or deadlifting 8000 pounds. Set intellectual goals like learning a language or pursuing a degree. Set goals for diet, sleep, and time/money management. Evaluate every day if your goals need to change and if you moved closer to them. Track major milestones for school, work, and competitions. Setting and achieving goals is a critical human pursuit. Make your goals hard to achieve. When you do achieve them, they will have more meaning.

3.0 PROFESSIONAL DEVELOPMENT

Being good at your job allows you to provide financially for you and your family, set an example for your children, and achieve your long-term objectives. Your professional success is key to your personal success.

3.1 PERFORMANCE

Being secure in your position at work
provides stability. Minimize the risk of
losing your job and the means to support
yourself or your family, by performing
well. Get better at your job each day and,
seek/take feedback from others when there
is an opportunity. Find ways to actively
support others and improve your team.

3.2 ADVANCEMENT/QUALIFICATIONS

Figure out what achievements are required
for promotion or advancement and take
deliberate steps to accomplish them.
Determine what certifications or
qualifications are required to outperform
your competition. Then earn them.

Find meaning in your job. If your job
doesn't have meaning, design an exit
strategy to move to one that does. A lot
of your time will be spent at work. Make
it matter.

4.0 CHARACTER/ LEADERSHIP

Who we are as a person is perhaps the most defining quality in our life. Our character impacts those around us and the world we live in and we are in complete control of it. Learning humility, managing our egos, and leading and mentoring people in our world are ways we can choose to develop our character. Remember, you don't need to be in charge of anyone or anything to lead. Everyone has the ability and the obligation to lead.

4.1 HUMILITY

This is the most important quality in a leader. Ego is the biggest killer in combat, business, and life. Be honest in your self-assessment of your own ego and control it. If your ego gets out of control, you will lose.

4.2 EMOTIONAL CONTROL

Everyone is emotional, but not everyone can control their emotions. You are not effective when you are emotional. You don't have productive conversations, send good emails, or make smart decisions when you lose control of our emotions. Know your red flags and learn to identify when emotions start to take over. Children struggle controlling their emotions. Eminently Qualified Humans do not.

4.3 MENTORING/CHARITY

Helping others. Having outlets to provide
support for those that need it in a way
that is productive for them. Set your best
example, mentor someone, help set goals
for friends and family members.

5.0 RELATIONSHIP

Relationships are your most powerful
tools for long term success. This is
true for everyone in life. You can't
accomplish much on your own and you need
people in your life if you are to reach
your fullest potential. Since time
available to spend with people is
limited, you need to get the most out of
every minute you have with them.

Interactions with family members should strengthen relationships, not weaken them.

Relationships with friends and co-workers should be built up at every opportunity.

Spending time with the people in your life should increase trust, esprit de corps, and mutual support.

6.0 PREPAREDNESS/ SAFETY

The world can be dangerous and bad things happen. Violence is a daily occurrence and can present itself without warning. You need to be prepared both physically and mentally and ensure the people closest to you are prepared as well. You need to train to effectively respond to a crisis.

6.1 MARTIAL ARTS/SELF-DEFENSE

Be able to protect yourself and your family
from physical violence.

6.2 WEAPONS TRAINING

Be able to protect your home from intruders
or intervene/escape correctly if required to
in public.

6.3 HOME SAFETY/EMERGENCY/DISASTER

Have a plan and ensure everyone in your home
executes that plan under stress.
Rehearse that plan and assess how
prepared your family is. Have all the
required equipment and supplies.
Everyone in your family should know CPR and
basic life-saving steps.

6.4 NEIGHBORHOOD/COMMUNITY IMPACT:

Develop relationships with other leaders in your neighborhood to protect against violence, disease, or disaster and create a safe environment for other residents.

THE EVALUATION

Most people are capable of getting better. Once they know the right attributes and understand what the parameters are and how to assess their performance, a lot more people will get closer to their goals.

Can we get actually there?

No, we can't.

Being eminently qualified isn't a status we achieve, or a conclusion we reach.

Being eminently qualified is being on The Path that does not end.

It's the way of living life where we accept that with every single day there is more to do.

The Eminently Qualified Human understands this and recognizes that no matter what measure of success has been achieved in one place, there is more to do elsewhere.

And as we shift our focus from one to the other, that success we just achieved will begin to erode, our gains will decay, and we will have to rebuild what we have lost.

The Eminently Qualified Human knows:

There is no end.

Since there is no stopping point on the quest to becoming an Eminently Qualified Human, what are we really trying to do?

The answer is simple:
We are trying to get better, every day.

This requires growth in every facet of personal and professional development.

This requires **ACTION**.

We have to turn our words into action.
We have to turn our ideas into action.
We have to turn our skills into action.
We have to turn our goals into action.

There are many resources out there that help us understand how we should behave, and what is important.

What we don't have is an evaluation system
for human beings that lets us define our
goal, identify the critical attributes
required to achieve it, and track our
progress along the way.

Until now.

Here is The Evaluation:

HEALTH

ATTRIBUTE	DESCRIPTION	SCORE: 0
PHYSICAL FITNESS	Activities that increase cardiovascular, strength, flexibility, and mobility. Daily actions that promote physical health.	Inactive. Did not perform any activities that contributed to my overall physical fitness level.
SLEEP/ REST	Understanding of optimal personal rest and sleep requirements and pursuit of daily actions that contribute to achieving them. Striking the right balance of those needs with the time demands of life.	Did not get rest or sleep that was useful in leading to a productive day. Slept so much or so little that the body was not capable of performing well.
DIET/ NUTRITION	Making healthy eating decisions based on an understanding of optimal nutrient intake. Consuming the ideal amount and type of calories at the right time to ensure optimal physical performance.	Did not eat properly and did not provide any nutritional benefit to perform critical daily tasks.

The daily routine of engaging in physical activity, rest, and nutrition to optimize the body to perform all the functions required to be a productive person.

SCORE: 1	SCORE: 2-4	SCORE: 5
Engaged in a basic fitness routine or activity.	Engaged in intense physical activity and demanding exercise that increased overall fitness level while addressing weaker areas that need improvement.	Participated in training that reached a level of exertion beyond my perceived limits. The most intense physical training that I was capable of performing set a new baseline for maximum useful effort.
Got minimal sleep or rest required to perform at the lowest acceptable standard throughout day.	Got effective sleep or rest throughout the day to be ready to perform at a high level.	Perfectly optimized body's need for rest. Went to sleep tired, woke up alert and ready after optimal number of hours asleep. Rested at the ideal time for the ideal duration to maintain a sustained peak level of performance throughout the entire day.
Food intake was effective to sustain health but did not optimize nutrition or participate in health enhancing program.	Made effective eating decisions throughout the day allowing for performance at a high level.	Consumed ideal food intake and maintained perfect adherence to diet or fasting. Every calorie was optimal, and nothing was consumed that didn't contribute to health and nutrition, allowing for a sustained peak level of performance throughout the entire day.

PERSONAL DEVELOPMENT

ATTRIBUTE	DESCRIPTION	SCORE: 0
INTELLECTUAL FITNESS	Activities and pursuits that contribute to increased learning, acquiring additional skills, and enhancing overall level of knowledge and ability. Involved in challenging artistic pursuits that develop often overlooked components of intellectual fitness.	Inactive. Did not engage in any activities that contributed to my overall mental fitness level.
TIME MANAGEMENT	Discipline applied to managing available time. Priority tasks are identified and accomplished in order, while avoiding anything that results in wasted time.	Wasted time today. Exerted no effort toward accomplishing anything productive.
FINANCIAL MANAGEMENT	Discipline applied to financial well being, income, savings, and growth. Making financial decisions and spending money that contributes to long term financial freedom.	Did not make financially intelligent decisions and was wasteful with money. Undermined goal of creating financial freedom.
PERSONAL GOALS	Ability to identify, clearly define, and establish a path to achieving worthwhile and meaningful goals. Accomplishment of the critical life events required to achieve those goals set for you and for the people influenced by you.	Spent no time considering new goals or missions. Remained comfortable with current plans and wasn't proactive in accomplishing anything useful.

The pursuit of activities and behaviors that develop the required attributes in your personal life that allows you to be productive, useful, and impactful.

SCORE: 1	SCORE: 2-4	SCORE: 5
Engaged in activities to sustain intellectual fitness. Read, wrote, etc in a way to maintain current level.	Took aggressive steps toward developing intellectual health. Read challenging books/articles, engaged in musical/artistic activities, escaped comfort zone.	Achieved a major breakthrough in understanding, grasped a concept that made significant impact to my life and my ability to impart knowledge and skills.
Managed time in a way that allowed me to accomplish the minimum required daily events.	Was highly productive and accomplished meaningful tasks throughout the day. Avoided distraction and time wasting activities.	Used every minute of the day to the max extent possible. Wasted no time and devoted energy to only the most critical and impactful priorities. Set standard for a new level of time management and productivity.
Made effort to be disciplined with money but made no contribution to future well being nor made a noteworthy improvement to future financial freedom.	Highly disciplined with money limiting wasteful spending.	Wasted no money, completely disciplined in spending and investing in only those things that will lead to long term financial freedom. Made decisions that will deliver lasting impact on me and my entire family, helping secure financial freedom.
Took time to consider minor goals. Worked toward achieving current goals without significant steps to create or achieve larger goals.	Significant movement toward reaching goal. Strong development of meaningful future goals.	Identified The Path and pursued goals that will lead to a better life. Completed one or more of the critical events required to achieve the standards I set for myself and for the people I influence.

PROFESSIONAL DEVELOPMENT

ATTRIBUTE	DESCRIPTION	SCORE: 0
PERFORMANCE	The skills and effort required to be effective at work and to ensure security and advancement in chosen career.	Performed work below the standard or did not work at all. Was counterproductive regarding individual and company wide success.
ADVANCEMENT/ QUALIFICATIONS	Identifying and accomplishing the required steps and professional education to increase responsibility and value to the organization.	Did nothing to move down The Path for increased growth and responsibility.

Productive, impactful, meaningful, and lucrative professional life. Pursuit of, and growth in, a career field that provides financial security and freedom, along with personal fulfillment and satisfaction.

SCORE: 1	SCORE: 2-4	SCORE: 5
Completed basic assigned tasks. Identified areas and tasks where additional guidance was needed in order to complete assignments, but did not perform in a note-worthy manner.	Exceeded standards established while completing key assignments accurately and on schedule. Helped others complete their assigned tasks.	Outperformed all expectations. Vastly exceeded requirements and set new standard for job perfor-mance. Completed all assignments ahead of schedule with a high degree of accuracy. Helped others complete their assigned tasks. Considered the impact of work up, down, and across the team and contributed fully to maximize it.
Pursued information regarding useful qualifications for my pro-fession. Sought out guidance and advice from others to determine how best to engage in the future.	Actively pursued professional cer-tifications and credentials. Sought out and implemented expert advice regarding additional higher level certifications.	Took most significant step toward achieving professional certifi-cations and credentials. Deeply involved with mentors regarding additional higher level certifi-cations and optimized path to achieving them.

CHARACTER/LEADERSHIP

ATTRIBUTE	DESCRIPTION	SCORE: 0
HUMILITY	Management of the ego that balances aggressive and difficult goals with behavior that cultivates the respect, loyalty, and support of those around you.	Allowed my ego to dictate my actions, undermining my credibility as a leader. Did not conduct a brutally honest self assessment or find ways to improve.
EMOTIONAL CONTROL	Ability to recognize and control counterproductive emotional responses. Recognizing weakness and having the ability to detach from emotion and react appropriately in difficult circumstances.	Lost control of emotions when interacting with the people around me during a stressful encounter. Set back any progress toward controlling emotions.
MENTORSHIP/ CHARITY	Identifying the need in others to be led. Demonstrating role model action and behavior that others can replicate to enhance their lives and the lives of the people around them. Being helpful and generous to people that need and can benefit from your help, while not encouraging long term dependency. Recognition of the benefit of helping those who are highly impacted by time spent with them.	Failed to provide a useful example when opportunities to do so were present. Did not hold myself to the standard. Gave nothing of my time, money, or energy to those in need.

Developing the traits and attributes required to earn the respect and support of the people in your world. Applying self-control to resist counterproductive human tendencies. Actions and behaviors that help the people around you win. Putting their success ahead of your own.

SCORE: 1	SCORE: 2-4	SCORE: 5
Stayed humble in normal life settings. Controlled my ego and maintained self awareness to it.	While in a situation where I normally allow my ego to dictate my actions, I maintained humility and behaved in an authentic and effective manner.	Controlled ego in the most challenging environment leading to an ideal outcome where previously I would have let my ego control me and make a bad decision. Actions created or reinforced my reputation as humble leader leading to significant increase in credibility and effectiveness as a leader.
Maintained control of my emotions in normal situations. Was aware of periods of heightened emotions and did not let them get out of control.	Maintained emotional control in difficult environments and used awareness of red flags to prevent emotions from getting out of control.	Maintained emotions under duress in the most difficult situation possible. Was able to immediately identify my own red flags or those of people around me, detach, and make the ideal decision to get the best possible outcome that otherwise would have been missed.
Found limited opportunity to help others. Made minimal impact when opportunities were present.	Made legitimate contribution to important people in my life needing support. Found an effective way to mentor/support someone that will make legitimate and lasting impact in their life.	Found a way to help someone in dire need that will benefit from my mentorship/charity in a way that impacts them and the world around them in the most profound way possible.

RELATIONSHIP

ATTRIBUTE	DESCRIPTION	SCORE: 0
QUALITY TIME WITH FAMILY	Strengthening relationships with your spouse, children, and other family members to build bonds and provide stability in their world by optimizing limited time available with family and friends.	Spent no time strengthening bonds with family. Missed opportunities to do something valuable with the people that matter most in my life.
QUALITY TIME FRIENDS/ CO-WORKERS	Recognizing the need for, and strengthening relationships outside your family by taking full advantage of the limited time available with friends and co-workers.	Spent no time strengthening bonds with friends. Missed opportunities to do something valuable with the important people in my life.

Developing and growing the relationships with the most important people in your world. Engaging in activities that strengthen those connections and allow those people to grow and improve because of their relationship with you. Making the most of the limited available time spent with the people most important to you.

SCORE: 1	SCORE: 2-4	SCORE: 5
Spent time with family but was distracted by other priorities and engaged in a limited way. Did not devote full attention to them.	Spent quality time with family. Maintained awareness of family schedule and major events in the lives of immediate family members so I could be present and contribute at a useful time.	Took full advantage of time spent with family and significantly strengthened those bonds. Made lasting contributions as a result of being fully aware of schedule and major events in the lives of family members.
Spent time with important friends but was distracted and engaged in a limited way. Did not offer full attention or engagement.	Spent quality time with friends/ co-workers. Found ways to be involved in major life events, positively impacting their life.	Took full advantage of time spent with the most important people outside my family and significantly strengthened those bonds. Fully aware of and engaged in important events leading to significant growth in relationships that will positively impact lives.

PREPAREDNESS/SAFETY

ATTRIBUTE	DESCRIPTION	SCORE: 0
MARTIAL ARTS	Training in legitimate fighting and grappling arts to be able to defend yourself or subdue an attacker when escape is not possible.	Did not train martial arts. Missed opportunities to study, observe, or train.
WEAPONS TRAINING	Training with legal weapons in your home and in public that contribute to safety for your community and the people around you.	Did not weapons train. Missed opportunities to study, observe, or train with weapons.
FIRE/SAFETY/ EMERGENCY	Owning and mastering the equipment and skills needed to respond to crises in your home. Training to keep family members safe during fire and emergency medical situations.	Did not acquire needed equipment and did not plan or rehearse emergency reactions. Allowed unacceptable level of unpreparedness to persist.
NEIGHBORHOOD/ COMMUNITY	Coordinating with other members of your neighborhood and creating vigilance that increases the overall safety, comfort, value, and security of your community.	Did not engage community or contribute to the well being of my neighborhood. Allowed opportunity to impact my community to be missed.

Identifying and preparing for the threats that exist to you, your family, and the people in your world. Recognizing the need to develop the skills, and possess the equipment required to respond to any emergency or threat in a safe and effective way.

SCORE: 1	SCORE: 2-4	SCORE: 5
Engaged in light/limited training to maintain proficiency but took no steps toward advancement.	Was part of aggressive training and significant learning that advanced my ability for self defense. Learned important new skills and techniques and made major improvement.	Made maximum effort toward mastery of new skill or technique that significantly increased ability for self defense. Entered a new phase of learning that profoundly increased control of my life and my ability to protect others.
Engaged in limited training to maintain proficiency but took no steps toward acquiring needed weapons nor advanced proficiency.	Participated in aggressive training and significant learning that advanced my weapons proficiency and comfort. Acquired new equipment and skills that enhanced self confidence and ability with self defense weapons.	Made a major advancement toward mastery of critical weapons that dramatically increased personal safety, safety of those around me, and preparedness to respond to a lethal threat in and out of home.
Acquired basic gear and equipment but did not train to its use or engage family on its use.	Acquired critical gear and equipment to make major increase in preparedness for all members of the house. Conducted training that advanced home safety, comfort with gear, and ability to respond to a crisis.	Acquired critical equipment to ensure home safety, completed a major rehearsal involving all members in a realistic setting, conducted training on vital life saving steps such as CPR and first aid, allowing me and everyone in my home to respond to crisis of any variety in the safest manner possible.
Made limited contribution in community matters.	Made a large contribution to important neighborhood event. Solved or assisted with a critical shortfall/need within the community which had gone unanswered to this point.	Led a critical and needed effort that made a major impact toward enhancing the safety and well being of the community. Behaved as the most impactful leader in my community, rallying those around me to make an increased level of contribution to the neighborhood and residents, leading to lasting impact.

THE EVALUATION...

is not designed just to grade yourself, but also so you know what you're trying to become.

It requires humility and a brutally honest self-assessment.

No one else is scoring you. Don't compare yourself to others.

This is about your capacity compared to your performance.

It is **you** against **you**.

Ask yourself how much effort you put into something and measure it against what you are capable of.

The more effort you put into something, the more progress you will make.

But this is different from person to person, and different for yourself as time goes on. If you've never exercised before in your life and you walk a mile, you may have exerted yourself close to your limit. That might be a 5. That same workout might be a 1 for someone who has been in the gym for years. But as you get better, and improve, that one mile walk no longer represents your maximum capacity so it's no longer a 5 for you.

As you move down The Path toward an Eminently Qualified Human, your capacity will increase. As a result, improving actually becomes more difficult over time. You have to work harder and do more to make the same amount — or even less — of an improvement.

This system only works if you understand what you're capable of and if you're honest about what you have done. Being easy on yourself doesn't help you or the people in your life.

You must commit.

You must stay on The Path.

WHAT DO YOU DO

You can and you will fall off The Path. It happens to everyone.

Sometimes, we do it to ourselves. Sometimes life hits us with something we didn't see coming.

People get sick. Accidents occur. Things happen in the world we can't control, and those things can push us off The Path.

But you can control how you react when you fall off. What you do to get yourself back on The Path is up to you.

The situation doesn't dictate what happens to you.

You dictate the situation.
You decide.

WHEN YOU FALL OFF THE PATH?

When you fall off The Path, ask yourself why. Why are you not doing the things you know you should? Do an unsparing self-assessment, identify corrective measures, and ruthlessly implement those measures.

TAKE ACTION. GET BACK ON THE PATH.
NOW.

For anything that affects the health of your mind or body, see your doctor or a professional in the field. This is not a time to rely on a friend or family member. You need professional help, so get it.

That being said, there are protocols to help you get back on The Path.

These are the Protocols:

SECTION 3

THE PROTOCOLS.

BREAKUP

My relationship is over and I don't know what to do.

1. Detach. Your emotions are your enemy during a break-up. They will not enable you to make good decisions or make good choices. Of course, this will be hard. The core of relationships is built on emotions. So, in order to detach from your emotions, take a step back. Look at the situation from someone else's point of view. You might think no one else understands — and you are right. They don't understand the emotions you have. But that means the emotions are not blinding them. Try to see that. If you have trouble detaching, go to step 1.a.

    a. It might also help to let your emotions out — but do so in a way that it does not affect the situation. Find a private place where you can scream, cry, or otherwise release your emotions. Try physically exerting yourself to get rid of emotional aggression. Hit a punching bag. Go for a run.

    b. Repeat step 1.a. as needed.

2. Assess the person you have separated from and evaluate who they actually are. The truth is, that person is not who you thought they were. The person you cared about does not exist. The idea that this person was a trustworthy faithful companion is not

true. You created an ideal around their framework, but that ideal did not actually exist. They have proven that ideal did not exist by their actions. Do not dwell on what it was, because it wasn't. Do not dwell on what it could have been, because it couldn't. It was a lie.

3.   Be thankful. Be thankful that this lie was uncovered now instead of later, before you invested even more into that person, that person who you now realize was not who you thought they were. Be thankful that you found out when you did that this person is untrustworthy. Be thankful that you can now move forward.

4.   Wish them luck. Yes. Perhaps it is a final conversation, perhaps it is a note. But wish them luck. They are going to need it. Do not harbor any ill feelings. Those ill feelings do you no good. Let them remember you not as a spiteful, vindictive slave to your emotions and whims, but as a good, mature person, ready to move on positively in the world.

5.   Walk away. You know this person is not who you wanted them to be and you can't change that. So, walk away. Move on.

6.   Don't look back. Your mind will play tricks on you. You will lie to yourself, tell yourself that "maybe it can work" and "maybe I was wrong" and "if I just try one more time, maybe he or she will change."

No. That is not happening. They aren't going to change. And the fact of the matter is, the more you crawl back to them, the more you belittle yourself and push them further away. Don't do it. Walk away. Don't look back.

7.   GET BACK ON THE PATH. Wake up early. Work out. Run. Read. Write. Learn. Play an instrument. Train jiu-jitsu. Eat clean. Clean your room. Clean your car. Get ahead at work. When someone breaks our trust, we question ourselves. We think our judgement is bad because we put our faith in this person who hurt us. So how do you build that trust back up with yourself? Look back and learn from the relationship. See the mistakes you made and the red flags you missed. Then look for them the next time around. Recognize that there are plenty of people out there in the world that are trustworthy and faithful. Go find one of them. Move forward in that relation- ship with a clean slate. Don't bring baggage.

DEATH

Someone I loved has died and I don't know how to deal with the loss.

1.   Accept that death is cruel, and it is not always fair. It is also inescapable and therefore death is part of life. Without death there is no life.

2.   Remember everything that person has given you during your time together - the experiences, the fun, and everything they have given you not only in their life but in their death. Remember the mark they left on you. Recognize the unforgettable precious moments you had together to know the beauty of their personality, their attitude, their outlook on the world.

3.   Take those memories and precious moments and write a eulogy for the person. You may or may not get to deliver that eulogy at their service depending on the situation. It doesn't matter. Write it anyway.

4.   Don't be selfish. Other people are experiencing the loss as well. It isn't about you. Do what you can to support the family of the individual who has died. If you are family, do what you can to support others in your family. Be strong.

5.   Understand the fact that you may lose control of your emotions during this time period. You will be

hit with powerful waves of emotions. You may want to cry; you may want to scream; you may want to shake your fists at the sky. When appropriate, let those emotions out. The waves will seem uncontrollable at first and they will come often. Over time those waves will be less powerful and come less often. That is okay. That doesn't mean you care less. It just means that you are gradually processing the loss. This is a good thing. Don't feel guilty about it. The person who died would not want you to be miserable.

6.   Know that you were lucky to have that person in your life, even if it was for too short of a time. Be thankful for the opportunity to have been with them. This person you lost has taught you that life is precious and how blessed we are to have every day to grow, to learn, to laugh, and to live.

7.   Write a letter to your lost loved one. Explain to them what they meant to you. Explain to them how they helped you and what they taught you. Tell them how you really felt about them. If there was friction between you, explain it. If you owe them an apology for something you said or did, apologize. Explain to them that you loved them and that you are going to miss them dearly and that you will never forget them. Explain that you will remember them, but you will not dwell in the past. Then explain to them that you are going to carry on with your life. That you are going to live your life — and promise them that you are going to live the best possible life you can and make them proud.

8.   Take the letter. Put it in an envelope. Write
their name on it. Bring it to their gravestone. Get
down on one knee. Put your hand on their grave. Place
the letter on the ground next to their gravestone.
Tell them you loved them and that you wrote them a
letter. Say goodbye. Then, go and *live*.

9.   Each year, on their birthday or on the day they
died, visit their grave. Bring flowers. Take a knee
and look at their gravestone. Read it aloud. Then
look at yourself and assess to see if you are
delivering on the promise you made to live the best
life you possible can and if they would be proud of
you.

MONEY PROBLEMS

I've lost my job, had an unexpected medical bill, a family emergency, unplanned travel, etc. and money is tight.

1.   Achieving financial freedom requires financial discipline which begins with tracking all of your financial activities. Start with a budget of all your income and expenses. You have to know where your money is going.

2.   Review past spending to see what is possible to reduce or eliminate. If you don't track your expenses, start doing it now. Get smart on basic financial planning and saving. Educate yourself.

3.   You may need to make aggressive and immediate decisions. Sell unneeded belongings and cancel services that are not necessary. Video game consoles and cable TV aren't requirements. Eat out less and eat at home more. Cancel your gym membership and start training in the garage. New clothes, vacations, or a new car will have to be put on hold.

4.   Continue to look for other ways to minimize your financial burden. Talk to your bank and renegotiate interest rates on any credit cards or loans. Pay off the highest interest rate loans as fast as possible and avoid additional debt. Take a second job or look for a higher paying position.

Devote more time to your current job to set yourself up for a raise or promotion. Do what you can to maximize income and minimize expenses.

5.   Don't keep your family in the dark. Get input from everyone affected by the situation and make it a team effort. Explain it so they realize this budget is not a punishment... it's the tool you are using to help everyone to achieve financial freedom and weather the storm. The more they understand the easier this will be.

6.   Review your budget every month, compare actual income and spending to the budget, and adjust accordingly. It might take time to dig yourself out of a financial hole, but with discipline, it will be achieved.

BETRAYAL OF TRUST

Someone betrayed me and I don't know what to do.

1.   Recognize that you just learned something about that person's character. You now know what you are dealing with and need to be alert around this person in the future.

2.   If this is a work situation and lives are at risk or if there is something happening that is morally or ethically wrong or illegal, then immediately confront the situation appropriately and escalate up the chain of command.

3.   Make sure you have evidence and don't go off half-cocked because people who are deceitful prepare and are ready for battle to protect themselves. They do not care what happens to other people - including you. They think they are getting away with their lies, so you must watch that person carefully.

4.   If there is major betrayal in your personal life, detach mentally, assess what it will take to disengage from this person. Take necessary steps and distance yourself from them.

5.   If the betrayal is minor, perhaps not even worthy of the word betrayal, then you log that in your brain and register that person as untrustworthy. You've seen their character. Noted. Know that you need to be

careful around them, because they think they're smarter than you and they can get away with it. But keep
that mistrust and dislike internal.

6.   You are a professional and you are emotionally
stable. Be diplomatic. Be tactful. Don't let anoth-
er human being's maneuvers get you worked up. Someone else should not get to control your emotions like
that. Stay in control.

PROBLEMS AT WORK

Everything is crashing around me — and I don't know what to do.

1.   Recognize that sometimes this is how life works. When things go wrong, they seem to happen all at once. They compound on top of each other and it is pretty easy sometimes to feel beaten when you are faced with all those issues and problems.

2.   Don't give up. In fact, do the opposite. It's time for you to fight harder. It's time to dig in and go on the warpath. That starts with one of the fundamental laws of combat leadership - **PRIORITIZE AND EXECUTE.**

3.   Make a list. What is the biggest problem? What is causing the most stress? Are your work pressures negatively impacting your home life?

4.   At home: Your family will likely pick up on your stress and tension from work. So, talk to your family - tell them the plan for how you are going to handle the situation and fix it. If you are going to be working longer hours make sure the family is aware of that and discuss and plan how everyone can help pick up any slack.

5.   At work: talk to your boss - face it. Tell him/ her that you are going to step up your game. Show up

early, work through lunch, stay late. Be wherever you need to be whenever they need you to be there. Explain that you are 100% committed to supporting the company, and the mission.

6.   With a coworker: It's time to have a professional discussion and work through any issues. Remember other people cannot read your mind. Your coworker may have no idea how they are impacting your work life and a simple conversation may make a dramatic improvement to the situation. Take ownership of the problem and listen to the other person with an open mind regarding your part in any work stress. Talk about what you are both going to do to improve the situation.

7.   It's going to be hard because life is hard. These challenges that you face will do their best to take you down. Do not let them. Stand up and dig in. Line up those problems and fight them. Let those challenges raise you up - elevate you. The trials and demands will make you stronger.

8.   Let the adversity you face today turn you into a better person tomorrow so in the future you look back at these struggles and you say "Thank You - you made me better".

APOLOGY

I said or did something that hurt someone's feelings and I need to make it right.

1.   Take Ownership of it. You are responsible for your words and actions. In most situations, a simple and honest "sorry" is sufficient. But sometimes you need to ask forgiveness.

2.   If saying sorry makes you feel uncomfortable spend some time thinking about why that is. Why did you hurt this person? How much do you care about this person? Is your ego preventing you from doing the right thing? Are you not humble enough to recognize that what you did was wrong?

3.   Find the right place and time to talk with the individual you want to apologize to. Late at night when everyone is tired or in a public place is not a good plan. Think about what you want to say and rehearse it. Be authentic but know what you're going to say. This is important.

4.   Avoid half apologies said with a tone that indicates you just want to get it over with and that you don't really mean it. It's not time to bring up past offenses that you are holding on to. Focus on the one situation and talk about that.

5.   If your children witnessed the argument where you hurt someone, let them know that you were wrong and that you asked for forgiveness. It's a teachable moment for them to see that apologizing and seeking forgiveness is a sign of strength not a sign of weakness.

6.   Control yourself in the future. Your goal should always be to retain control of your words and actions so that you preserve your relationships. But if you lost that control remember that the path forward to restoring your relationship begins with you.

ACCIDENT/ILLNESS

How do I move forward after an accident or severe medical diagnosis?

1.   The fight is not over - in fact it has just begun. Cancer diagnosis? Accident with serious injuries? It's time to put aside anything that is not aimed directly towards your full effort on beating the diagnosis or learning to adapt to your new circumstances. Understand this might take time, possibly years to heal or adapt.

2.   You are alive right now. It's time to fight. Prepare yourself for the long war.

3.   Your first move should be to get help. Gather all the tools you can to fight - doctors, family, friends, and any resources that will aid in your recovery. Build a plan and then work the plan with discipline and belief.

4.   You need a counterpart in this battle. Someone you can count on. Someone that will ask tough questions and give straight answers to you and to your doctors — to your family. It could be a family member, a friend, or a coworker. Their main quality needs to be speaking the truth. The more time they can be by your side the better.

5.   Get organized. There will be paperwork, appointments, prescriptions, bills, and countless other details that need to be tracked. **TRACK THEM**. Make a system. Use it.

6.   Talk with your work. Explain your situation. Ask for help. Utilize their resources if they have any.

7.   You're going to need help, and people will offer it. Use it, but remember, that the logistics of the support mechanisms can get overwhelming. From the people that offer help, get one of them to take lead of the support team.

8.   Know that you can win. You can come out even stronger because you now know real darkness, and now truly appreciate the light.

9.   Focus on beating this and no matter the outcome you will know you did everything in your power to **Fight and WIN** and that is a victory in itself.

ADDICTION

I am addicted to a substance, activity, or something that controls me, and I don't know how to break it.

Dealing with this addiction may require professional help. If that is the case, get it now. Do not let your ego get in the way of getting the help you need.

1.   Admit that you are controlled by something external in your life. This thing makes your life worse, not better, and prevents you from reaching your fullest potential. You cannot become what you are capable of until you beat this.

2.   Don't blame others or accept that you are a victim — take full responsibility of the situation.

3.   Write down everything bad that comes from this. Calculate the cost financially, emotionally, mentally, physically, and the impact on your relationships because of your addiction.

4.   Then write down everything good that comes from it.

5.   Now write down the long-term outcome of maintaining this addiction. What effects will this have on your life in the end and how do you see the people in the world being affected by this?

6.   Build a plan to stop. This is something you can do, and you can control. But again, you may need professional help. Do not underestimate your need for support. If professional help is required, get it.

7.   Master this plan. Commit to the steps required to win and be disciplined in following them every day.

8.   Separate yourself from your addiction. Avoid people who enable your addiction and don't want to see you defeat it. Surround yourself with people who want to see you win.

9.   When the urge to feed your addiction strikes, discipline yourself with exercise, reading, writing, or anything else that prevents you from falling off The Path again.

10. If you do fall off The Path again, get back on it.

11. Do what is necessary. You know the answer and you know what to do. You are 100% in control of your own actions.

TRAUMA

I suffered a psychological trauma and I don't know how to deal with it.

Dealing with this trauma may require professional help. If that is the case, get it now. Do not let your ego get in the way of getting the help you need.

1.   Accept that you were affected by a serious event that has had a real psychological impact on your life.

2.   Don't accept that you are a victim - this may be a difficult situation, but you have control over how you respond to the trauma.

3.   Write down everything bad that came from the trauma. Consider the impact it has had on your life, the damage it has done to you physically, mentally, and emotionally. Acknowledge where you are right now because of what happened.

4.   Write down everything good that came from it.

    a.   Has it made you appreciate what you had before?

    b.   Has it made you realize it could have been worse?

c. Do you see that others have endured worse?

d. Has it shown you that there is resilience and strength inside of you?

5. Avoid behaviors that are counterproductive. Don't drink, don't do drugs. Don't look for ways to avoid or numb the pain.

6. Build a disciplined schedule. Wake up early and exercise. Eat healthy, work hard, spend quality time with your family, friends, and important people in your life.

7. And when you feel like those people don't understand, you're right, they don't.

8. It's ok, because you understand. Don't avoid the darkness, don't ignore it.

9. You know darkness. And because of that, you know light.

10. Set out on a path toward the light. Find joy, laughter, sun, exercise, and nature.

11. Don't let this trauma beat you or take that away from you. Move forward every day.

12. Beat this trauma by living your life.

THE UNKNOWN

What do I do when I don't know what to do? Something bad happened and I don't even know where to start.

This is the strategy protocol. Every scenario cannot be addressed so this is the protocol for what to do when you don't know what to do.

1.   Start by taking a step back. Detach. Take a breath and look around. Make sure you assess everything that is happening.

2.   Think about what your possibilities are and what decisions you could make RIGHT NOW and what are the likely outcomes of those decisions.

3.   Write it down. What does success look like in this situation? How can you get there? How long should it take? Do you know anyone who can provide guidance or advice?

4.   Work the plan. Take action that moves you forward. Don't stay stagnant. Don't dwell. Take a small step towards what you think is the best decision. Not a giant step - because you don't know exactly what is going on. This is a step that allows you to assess again before you decide what to do next.

5.   Push forward then pause and reassess again. Repeat and press forward to the point of friction. Press until you reach the point where you see a new opportunity or a need to pull back and reassess again.

6.   Allow yourself room to maneuver. When it gets hard — don't surrender, don't give up, don't quit. Then you haven't failed. All it means is you need to regroup and reattack. You've learned, you've gained experience, and **YOU ARE STILL ALIVE.**

HOW TO HANDLE

You are on The Path. You are seeing the results of your hard work and your efforts are paying off. Unmitigated Daily Discipline in all things is not just a saying - it's your life.

Your health is excellent, work and personal performance is exceeding expectations, you are leading in all aspects of your life.

So, what now?

Thank those who helped you along the way. Take stock in what you have achieved.

SUCCESS WHILE ON THE PATH

Then go harder.

Lead.

Lead your family, your community, your Country. Lead everyone and everything in your world.

Lead others to The Path. Show them The Way.

Unmitigated Daily

Discipline

in all things.

It is the only Way.

Track your progress with downloadable
Evaluation forms at:

jockopublishing.com/downloads

Made in the USA
Middletown, DE
28 April 2020

92367136R00053